WEYMOUTH

Travel Guide 2024

A Guide to Sun, Culture, Must See
Attractions, Hidden Gems and Thrilling
Adventures in Dorset's Coastal City

Wendy T. Sierra

Copyright

Table of Contents

Forward

Welcome to **"Weymouth Travel Guide 2024."** As someone who has fallen deeply in love with this charming coastal town, I am thrilled to share with you the magic that makes Weymouth such a special destination.

My journey with Weymouth began several years ago during a spontaneous weekend trip. What started as a brief escape from the hustle and bustle of city life quickly turned into an enduring affection for this quaint seaside gem. I remember my first morning walk along Weymouth Beach, the sun rising over the calm waters, casting a golden glow on the sands. The tranquillity of that moment, coupled with the warm, welcoming vibe of the town, was simply unforgettable.

Weymouth is a place where history meets natural beauty, where you can wander through centuries-old forts in the morning and relax by the water's edge in the afternoon. My explorations led me to the historic Nothe Fort, where I felt transported back in time as I walked through its storied halls. Yet, it was the simple pleasures, like enjoying fresh seafood by the harbour or watching boats glide gently through the marina, that truly captured my heart.

One of my favourite discoveries was Bennetts Water Gardens. Strolling through its peaceful pathways, surrounded by the vibrant colours of water lilies, was a serene experience that remains etched in my memory. And then there were the spontaneous adventures – like taking a boat trip along the dramatic Jurassic Coast, marvelling at the natural rock formations and uncovering the prehistoric secrets hidden within.

This guide is designed to help you experience the very best of Weymouth, from its iconic landmarks and bustling markets to its tranquil parks and thrilling outdoor activities. It is a culmination of my personal experiences, countless conversations with locals, and the joy of discovering new corners of this enchanting town.

Whether you are visiting for the first time or returning to explore more, I hope this guide inspires you to delve deeper, to uncover the hidden gems, and to create your own unforgettable memories in Weymouth. Here's to a journey filled with adventure, relaxation, and the warmest of welcomes. Enjoy every moment of your stay in this wonderful corner of Dorset.

Introduction

Overview of Weymouth

Weymouth, located on the picturesque Jurassic Coast in Dorset, England, is a delightful coastal town known for its beautiful sandy beaches, busy port, and rich history. Weymouth, a popular destination for both visitors and locals, provides an ideal balance of natural beauty and cultural activities. The town's gorgeous backdrop, with its clear seas and colourful beach cottages, welcomes tourists to unwind and take in the tranquil coastal ambiance. Weymouth has something for everyone, whether you want to see historical sites, participate in water sports, or simply relax by the sea.

History and Heritage

Weymouth's history is as compelling as its stunning views. The town's history may be traced back to the Roman era, but it genuinely developed during the mediaeval period, when it became an important port. The Black Death is said to have reached England via Weymouth in the 14th century, marking an important period in the town's history.

In the 18th century, King George III's repeated trips to Weymouth promoted the town as a coastal resort, bringing wealth and expansion. The Esplanade, with its Georgian architecture, is a testimony to this era, highlighting the town's exquisite heritage. Another historical relic that reflects Weymouth's military history is the Nothe Fort, which was erected in the nineteenth century to safeguard the port. Today, tourists may explore these historical monuments and more, immersing themselves in Weymouth's rich history.

Getting to Weymouth

Weymouth is easily accessible by numerous kinds of transportation, making it a great place for a stress-free vacation.

Weymouth is well-connected by train, with regular connections to London, Bristol, and other important cities. The journey from London Waterloo takes around 2.5 hours and includes a picturesque tour through the countryside. The train station is within walking distance of the town centre, making it simple to begin your experience upon arrival.

By Car: Those who prefer to drive can reach Weymouth via the A354 from Dorchester. The drive provides beautiful scenery and the freedom to explore neighbouring sights at your own speed. There is plenty of parking accessible around town, including long-term parking lots for lengthy stays.

By Bus: National Express and other coach companies run frequent routes to Weymouth from various points around the UK. The bus station is strategically positioned, allowing for easy access to the town's services and attractions.

By Air: The nearest airports are Bournemouth and Exeter, both around an hour apart from Weymouth. To get to town from the airport, you can either rent a vehicle or utilise public transit.

By Water: Weymouth's harbour can handle private boats and yachts, making it convenient for people going by water. The harbour's amenities include mooring areas and needed services for sailors.

When to Visit

Weymouth is a year-round resort, with each season bringing its own distinct charm and activities. However, the optimum time to come is determined on your interests and the activities you intend to undertake during your stay.

Spring (March to May): Spring is an excellent season to visit Weymouth since the weather begins to warm and the town blooms. This season is ideal for visiting gardens, walking trails, and participating in outdoor activities without the summer crowds. Spring festivals and events add to the colourful ambiance, making it a great time for a calm but exciting break.

Summer (June to August) is the biggest tourist season in Weymouth, and for good reason. The warm weather and long days make the ideal setting for beach trips, water sports, and outdoor activities. Weymouth Beach comes alive with families, sunbathers, and swimmers, and the port is bustling with activity. If you want a lively, festive environment and don't mind crowds, summer is the perfect season to see the town at its most dynamic.

Autumn (September to November): Weymouth's pleasant weather and fewer tourists make it an ideal time for a more relaxing vacation. The changing foliage adds beauty to the terrain, and it's a great time to go hiking, cycling, or exploring the outdoors. Autumn events, such as the Dorset Seafood Festival, provide cultural and gastronomic experiences to enjoy.

Winter (December to February): Weymouth is calmer, providing a serene escape with a Christmas twist. While the weather has cooled, the town's charm remains, with comfortable taverns, seasonal events, and possibilities for brisk beach walks. The Christmas lights and seasonal markets create a magnificent ambiance, making it the ideal time for a winter getaway.

Regardless of when you arrive, Weymouth's warm atmosphere, rich history, and breathtaking natural beauty assure a great stay. Whether you're drawn to the lively summer sights or the tranquil winter settings, Weymouth is a place that will amaze and please.

Where to Stay

Finding the ideal location to stay is an important aspect of any enjoyable holiday, and Weymouth has a variety of lodgings to suit every taste and budget. Whether you want luxury, a quaint bed and breakfast, a family-friendly resort, or a low-cost choice, Weymouth has something for everyone.

Luxury Hotels

For visitors seeking a luxurious stay, Weymouth boasts numerous high-end hotels that provide great service, exquisite accommodations, and top-notch facilities.

Moonfleet Manor: A magnificent family-friendly hotel located in a beautiful Georgian manor home with views of Chesil Beach and the Fleet Lagoon. The hotel offers nicely designed rooms, an indoor pool, spa services, and gourmet cuisine. With its lovely setting and outstanding service, it's ideal for a relaxed and pleasant stay.

The Alexandra Hotel: This boutique hotel blends modern comfort with historical charm. The Alexandra Hotel, on Weymouth Beach, has nicely designed rooms with sea views, an on-site restaurant providing locally produced food, and a calm garden. Its central position offers it an excellent base for exploring Weymouth.

The Riviera Hotel: The Riviera Hotel, located on Bowleaze Cove, has Art Deco architecture and a variety of exquisite amenities, including a heated indoor pool, spa services, and a well-regarded restaurant. The hotel's distinct style and picturesque setting make it an excellent choice for a luxury break.

Boutique Bed and Breakfasts

Staying at one of Weymouth's lovely bed and breakfasts provides a more intimate and customised experience. These motels provide comfortable rooms, friendly service, and great home-cooked breakfasts.

The Roundhouse: This one-of-a-kind, circular bed and breakfast has breathtaking views of Weymouth Bay and the port. Each room is carefully furnished and equipped with contemporary facilities. The Roundhouse's central location and friendly environment make it a popular choice for couples and lone travellers.

Harlequin Guest House: Located just a short walk from the beach, Harlequin Guest House offers comfortable accommodations and a welcoming, calm atmosphere. Each morning, guests may enjoy a full breakfast made with locally sourced ingredients. The guest house's handy location makes it simple to visit Weymouth's attractions.

St. John's Guest House: This beautifully renovated Victorian guest house has spacious, nicely designed rooms and serves a superb breakfast buffet. St. John's Guest House is ideal for guests seeking comfort and convenience, since it is accessible to both the beach and the town centre.

Family-Friendly Resorts

Weymouth is an excellent family vacation location, with various resorts catering exclusively to families with children, providing a variety of activities and services to keep everyone entertained.

Haven Littlesea Holiday Park: This popular holiday park has a range of accommodations, including caravans and lodges. Indoor and outdoor pools, a kids' club, sports activities, and nightly entertainment are among the amenities available on site. The park's beachfront setting and family-friendly attractions make it an ideal destination for a fun-filled family holiday.

Waterside Vacation Park & Spa: Situated near Bowleaze Cove, this vacation park provides contemporary caravans and lodges, many of which have beautiful sea views. The resort has indoor and outdoor pools, a spa, restaurants, and a variety of activities for both children and adults. Its extensive amenities and gorgeous surroundings make it perfect for families.

Seaview Holiday Park: Another great alternative for families, Seaview Holiday Park has a variety of comfortable rooms and activities to keep everyone entertained. The park has swimming pools, sports courts, a playground, and family entertainment activities. Its relaxing environment and family-friendly amenities provide a comfortable stay for everybody.

Budget-Friendly Option

Weymouth offers a variety of economical lodging alternatives, including budget hotels, hostels, and self-catering flats.

Premier Inn Weymouth Seafront: This popular budget hotel company provides clean, comfortable rooms at a reasonable price. Weymouth Seafront is conveniently located near the beach and other local attractions. Guests will appreciate the on-site restaurant and the convenience of the central location.

YHA Portland: For those who prefer a hostel experience, YHA Portland provides affordable lodgings with breathtaking views of the coast. The hostel offers both private and dormitory-style rooms, as well as self-catering options and a community area. It's an excellent choice for lone travellers, backpackers, and groups.

Weymouth Sands Guest Home: This low-cost guest home provides simple but pleasant accommodations and courteous service. Weymouth Sands Guest House, located near the beach and town centre, offers superb value for money and serves as a great base for exploring the region.

Finally, Weymouth provides a varied choice of hotels to meet the interests and tastes of all travellers. Whether you want to indulge in luxury, experience the beauty of a bed and breakfast, discover a family-friendly resort, or stay on a budget, this gorgeous seaside town has the right spot to stay for a great trip.

Iconic Landmarks

Weymouth is full of magnificent landmarks that grab the hearts of everyone who visits. From its beautiful sandy beaches to its mediaeval defences, each location provides a unique peek into the town's dynamic personality and rich history. Whether you're a history enthusiast, a nature lover, or just looking for a beautiful place to unwind, Weymouth's monuments provide limitless chances for discovery and enjoyment.

Weymouth Beach

Weymouth Beach is one of the town's most popular attractions, enticing visitors with its golden sands and calm, shallow waves. The beach, which stretches three miles down the coastline, provides an ideal backdrop for leisure and entertainment. Its family-friendly atmosphere makes it ideal for youngsters to play, create sandcastles, and swim in the safe waters. Lifeguards are on duty during peak seasons to ensure a safe environment for all beachgoers.

The esplanade next to the beach is a lovely promenade dotted with attractive cafés, ice cream stands, and classic seaside attractions. Visitors may take a leisurely stroll down the esplanade and enjoy breathtaking views of the coast as well as hectic beach activities. For those seeking more energetic hobbies, the beach provides a range of water sports such as kayaking, paddleboarding, and windsurfing. Weymouth Beach offers all desires, whether you want to relax in the sun, go swimming, or participate in exciting water activities.

Weymouth Harbour

Weymouth Harbour is a scenic and dynamic location that embodies the town's maritime past. The harbour, with its colourful fishing boats and luxurious yachts, is a thriving hive of activity. Walking around the harborfront, tourists may see fishermen unloading their catch of the day, giving a true touch of local life to the gorgeous sights.

The waterfront is dotted with restaurants, ranging from traditional fish and chip shops to fine dining establishments, serving the freshest seafood and a wide range of gastronomic pleasures. Outdoor seating allows visitors to relish their meals while taking in the harbour's attractiveness.

The unique lifting bridge that connects the two sides of the harbour is an impressive sight. Watching the bridge rise to allow boats to sail through is an unforgettable experience that adds to the harbour's appeal. Furthermore, the port holds a variety of events throughout the year, such as seafood festivals, regattas, and music concerts, making it a vibrant and interesting location for visitors.

Nothe Fort

Nothe Fort, located on a hill above Weymouth Harbour, is a historic monument that provides an intriguing peek into the town's military history. Built in the nineteenth century to safeguard the port, the fort is an extraordinary edifice with labyrinthine tunnels, reinforced walls, and breathtaking panoramic views of the coastline.

Visitors to Nothe Fort may explore its huge network of underground corridors and rooms, each containing intriguing displays on the fort's history and role in coastal defence. The fort's museum displays a variety of military objects, including weapons and uniforms as well as historical papers and pictures, offering a thorough account of the area's military legacy.

The fort's exterior spaces are appealing, with well-kept gardens and vantage points that provide panoramic views of Weymouth Bay and the surrounding environs. Nothe Gardens, close to the fort, is a quiet refuge ideal for a leisurely walk or picnic, with rich foliage and breathtaking panoramas. Seasonal events, such as reenactments and guided tours, improve the tourist experience, making Nothe Fort a must-see destination for both history buffs and casual visitors.

Jurassic Skyline

The Jurassic Skyline is a must-see for amazing vistas and a unique viewpoint on Weymouth and its gorgeous coastline. This observation tower, also known as the Weymouth Tower, stands 174 feet tall and offers a 360-degree panoramic view over the town, Jurassic Coast, and beyond.

The journey begins with a mild ascent in the spinning gondola, which provides a steadily increasing perspective as it rises. Once at the summit, tourists are rewarded with breathtaking views, with clear days displaying panoramas as far as Portland Bill, Chesil Beach, and the Isle of Purbeck. The tower's comprehensive audio commentary highlights significant areas of interest and explains the geological and historical significance of the surrounding area.

The Jurassic Skyline provides a fantastic opportunity to observe the region's natural splendour and different sceneries. The revolving gondola ensures that all angles are covered, providing a thorough and breathtaking perspective of Weymouth and its surroundings. Whether you're a photographer looking for the ideal snap or simply want to have a peaceful and gorgeous experience, the Jurassic Skyline provides a wonderful and fulfilling visit.

In summary, these prominent sites capture the spirit of Weymouth, combining natural beauty, rich history, and vibrant local culture. Weymouth Beach promotes relaxation and pleasure, Weymouth Harbour delivers a bustling and genuine seaside experience, Nothe Fort explores the town's history, and the Jurassic Skyline provides stunning views.

Each monument adds to Weymouth's distinct appeal, transforming it into a destination that grabs the hearts and imaginations of all visitors.

Museums & Galleries

Weymouth's rich history and culture are well represented in its many museums and galleries. Each site provides a unique glimpse into the town's past and present, encouraging visitors to explore, learn, and be inspired. Weymouth's cultural institutions offer engaging experiences for people of all ages, including intriguing historical items and stunning art displays. Dive into this chapter to learn about Weymouth's stories, art, and legacy.

Weymouth Museum

Weymouth Museum provides an intriguing trip through the town's rich history, reflecting the essence of its maritime heritage and dynamic past. The museum, housed in Brewers Quay, a historic structure that was formerly a brewery, is a treasure mine of antiques, pictures, and displays that give a vivid picture of Weymouth's growth over the years.

The museum's holdings range from ancient to present times, emphasising important events and ordinary life in Weymouth. Visitors may see exhibits on the town's Roman roots, role in the Black Death, and metamorphosis into a prominent coastal resort during the Georgian and Victorian eras. Maritime aficionados will especially like the exhibitions on Weymouth's nautical past, which feature ship models, navigational instruments, and stories of heroic sea experiences.

The museum's interactive displays and activities attract visitors of all ages, making it an ideal educational resource for both families and history aficionados. Whether you're interested in archeology, local legends, or maritime history, Weymouth Museum offers a detailed and engaging look at the town's past.

Tudor House Museum

Visit the Tudor House Museum, a wonderfully preserved 17th-century building that depicts household life throughout the Tudor and Stuart periods. This ancient house, located in the centre of Weymouth, is a unique jewel that offers an intimate glimpse into how people used to live, work, and socialise.

The museum's rooms are painstakingly decorated with period-appropriate furniture, fabrics, and domestic goods, resulting in a realistic setting. Each room conveys a unique tale, from the kitchen with its traditional cooking tools to the pleasant parlour with exquisite tapestries and wooden furnishings. Knowledgeable guides are available to share information and tales about the house's history and the individuals who have lived there.

Special activities and reenactments bring history to life, allowing visitors to witness traditional crafts, cooking demonstrations, and period costumes. The Tudor House Museum is a delightful and instructive site ideal for anyone who values history and enjoys learning about it in a hands-on, engaging way.

Leighton Art Gallery

The Leighton Art Gallery, a modern gallery that exhibits the works of local and regional artists, will appeal to art aficionados. Located in a charming area of Weymouth, the gallery offers a dynamic environment for artistic expression and cultural enrichment.

The gallery's shows include a variety of mediums, such as paintings, sculptures, ceramics, and photography. Regularly changing exhibitions guarantee that there is always something fresh and fascinating to view, with a focus on showcasing the abilities and inventiveness of Dorset-based artists. The gallery also offers art seminars and classes, giving visitors the opportunity to connect with art on a deeper level and maybe even create their own masterpieces.

The Leighton Art Gallery promotes a warm and inclusive environment, inviting both art enthusiasts and casual visitors to explore its collections and participate in its programs. Whether you're a seasoned collector or simply like beautiful and thought-provoking art, the gallery is a delightful destination to add to your Weymouth itinerary.

Sandsfoot Castle and Gardens

Sandsfoot Castle, an ancient ruin overlooking the sea, has a distinct combination of history, architecture, and natural beauty. Henry VIII built the castle in the 16th century as part of his coastal fortifications; now, it stands as a charming relic of the past, surrounded by wonderfully kept gardens.

Although the castle's remnants have been battered by time and the elements, they nonetheless emanate majesty and historical significance. Informational plaques give context and background, allowing visitors to envisage what the castle would have looked like in its prime and comprehend its significance in guarding the coast from prospective attackers.

The neighbouring Sandsfoot Gardens are a serene retreat, with vivid flower beds, groomed lawns, and peaceful seating spaces overlooking Portland Harbour and the Jurassic Coast. The grounds are great for a leisurely stroll, a picnic, or simply sitting and enjoying the peaceful surroundings.

Sandsfoot Castle and Gardens also offer a variety of community events and outdoor concerts, which contribute to its popularity as a cultural and recreational attraction. Sandsfoot Castle and Gardens is a must-see for anybody visiting Weymouth due to its historical significance and natural beauty.

Finally, Weymouth's museums and galleries provide a diverse range of cultural experiences, each with its own viewpoint on the town's history, art, and legacy. Weymouth Museum explores the town's complex past, Tudor House Museum brings history to life with historical settings, Leighton Art Gallery promotes modern inventiveness, and Sandsfoot Castle and Gardens combine history and natural beauty. Together, these sites form a full and fascinating cultural itinerary for Weymouth tourists.

Parks & Nature Reserves

Weymouth is not just a coastal destination with beautiful beaches and historical sites, but it is also a nature lover's paradise. The town is filled with lovely parks and wildlife reserves that provide a peaceful respite from the rush and bustle of daily life. These open places are ideal for leisurely walks, picnics, animal viewing, and simply enjoying the great outdoors. Weymouth has something for any nature enthusiast, whether it's a family-friendly park, a tranquil garden, or a thriving wildlife reserve.

Lodmoor Country Park

Lodmoor Country Park is a dynamic and diversified green park located within a short distance from Weymouth's town centre. The park, which covers more than 350 acres, provides a variety of activities and attractions, making it an ideal destination for families, nature lovers, and outdoor enthusiasts.

One of the park's features is its vast meadows and wetlands, which are home to a diverse range of animals. Birdwatchers will enjoy observing kingfishers, herons, and a variety of waterfowl that live in the vicinity. The park's well-kept walking and cycling pathways give easy access to various natural areas, allowing visitors to explore and relax in the peaceful surroundings.

Lodmoor Country Park provides a range of leisure opportunities for individuals who enjoy more physical hobbies. The park has a huge adventure playground where youngsters may burn off energy, as well as a popular pitch and putt golf course. The park also includes the Weymouth Sea Life Adventure Park, where visitors may learn about marine life and participate in interactive displays.

Throughout the year, Lodmoor Country Park holds a variety of events and festivals, contributing to its lively atmosphere. This lively green space hosts a variety of events, including outdoor concerts, wildlife walks, and educational programs. Whether you want to relax in nature or participate in outdoor activities, Lodmoor Country Park has something for everyone.

Radipole Lake Nature Reserve

Radipole Lake Nature Reserve is a hidden treasure in the middle of Weymouth that provides a calm respite from the town's hustle and bustle. The RSPB (Royal Society for the Protection of Birds) manages this urban wetland reserve, which serves as a wildlife refuge as well as a peaceful environment for tourists.

The reserve is well-known for its diverse wildlife, which draws visitors from all around. There have been over 200 bird species documented here, including bitterns, marsh harriers, and bearded tits. Visitors may explore the different ecosystems, which include reed beds, open water, and wet meadows, via a network of pathways and boardwalks. Observation hides strategically located around the area offer great view points for bird observation and photography.

Radipole Lake is home to a diverse range of animals, including otters, water voles, and dragonflies. The reserve's visitor centre has informational displays, guided tours, and children's activities, making it an instructive and exciting destination for visitors of all ages.

Radipole Lake periodically hosts seasonal events and nature-themed activities, giving guests the opportunity to learn about conservation and the necessity of maintaining wetland ecosystems. Radipole Lake Nature Reserve is a must-see site in Weymouth, whether you're an experienced birdwatcher or just searching for a tranquil area to reconnect with nature.

Bennetts Water Garden

Bennetts Water Gardens is a peaceful and attractive destination on the outskirts of Weymouth, famed for its breathtaking water lily displays and wonderfully maintained gardens. The gardens, which span eight acres, provide a peaceful respite as well as a sensory delight.

Bennetts Water Gardens' main attraction is its collection of water lilies, which bloom abundantly throughout the summer months. The gardens include one of the largest collections of water lilies in the country, with types imported from all around the world. The sight of these vivid blossoms floating on the surface of the ponds is simply stunning, with several photo opportunities.

In addition to the water lilies, the gardens have other themed areas, such as a Japanese garden, a Mediterranean garden, and a forest garden. Each area is painstakingly constructed and maintained, with a wide variety of flora and sceneries to explore. Winding walkways and tiny bridges guide visitors through the gardens, giving new vistas and surprises at each turn.

Bennetts Water Gardens also houses a museum dedicated to the history and production of water lilies, which offers unique insights into these stunning plants. A delightful café overlooking the grounds provides a pleasant setting to sip refreshments while admiring the sights.

Bennetts Water Gardens hosts special events, workshops, and guided tours throughout the year, making it a vibrant and interesting destination for both garden aficionados and casual visitors. Bennetts Water Gardens provides a lovely and inspirational experience for horticulturists as well as those seeking a tranquil spot to rest.

Greenhill Garden

Greenhill Gardens is a popular public garden on Weymouth's beachfront, with beautiful views of Weymouth Bay and a variety of flower displays. This award-winning garden is a popular destination for both residents and visitors, offering the ideal combination of beauty, relaxation, and leisure.

The gardens are well-known for their beautifully managed flower beds, which include a diverse range of seasonal flowers that provide a vivid and colourful display year-round. Visitors may stroll around the gardens and enjoy the sight and aroma of roses, lavender, and other flowering plants that have been beautifully placed to create visual beauty.

Greenhill Gardens also has various well-designed amenities, such as a café, a putting green, and a tennis court, making it an excellent choice for recreational activities. Throughout the summer, the gardens' bandstand presents live music performances on a regular basis, adding to the vibrant and pleasant environment.

Greenhill Gardens' placement on the seafront makes it an ideal stop for tourists visiting Weymouth's shoreline. The gardens' benches and lounging spaces are ideal for relaxing and taking in the panoramic views of the bay, while the neighbouring Greenhill Beach provides a tranquil environment for a beach promenade.

Greenhill Gardens hosts a variety of events and activities, including garden tours and family-friendly workshops, ensuring that there is always something fresh to explore. Whether you want to take a leisurely walk, participate in recreational activities, or simply appreciate the beauty of the surroundings, Greenhill Gardens is a must-see site in Weymouth.

In summary, Weymouth's parks and nature reserves provide a variety of activities, each offering a unique opportunity to interact with nature and enjoy the outdoors. Lodmoor Country Park is a bustling centre of activity and animals, Radipole Lake Nature Reserve provides a tranquil wetland getaway, Bennetts Water Gardens enchants with its water lilies and vistas, and Greenhill Gardens charms with flower displays and coastal charm. Together, these green places provide a rich and varied natural tapestry that adds to Weymouth's charm.

Outdoor Activities

Weymouth's stunning landscapes and maritime charm make it an ideal destination for outdoor lovers. Whether you're an adrenaline seeker searching for thrilling water sports, a nature lover hoping to discover cycling and walking paths, a fisherman looking for the perfect fishing place, or a golf enthusiast, Weymouth offers something for you. Explore the great outdoors and discover the many activities that make Weymouth a top location for adventure and leisure.

Water Sports and Sailing

Weymouth's position on the Jurassic Coast makes it an excellent destination for a range of watersports and sailing activities. Whether you're a seasoned enthusiast or a newbie eager to try something new, Weymouth's waters provide something for everyone.

The town's protected harbour provides ideal sailing conditions, making it a popular destination for sailors of all abilities. The Weymouth and Portland National Sailing Academy, which hosted the sailing events at the 2012 Olympics, has excellent facilities and training programs. You may take lessons, rent equipment, and participate in sailing regattas and tournaments all year.

Weymouth has a variety of watersports opportunities, including windsurfing, kitesurfing, and paddleboarding. The consistent breezes and tranquil waters provide an ideal setting for these pursuits. Several local schools and rental businesses provide instruction and equipment, ensuring that you have all you need for an exciting day on the lake.

Kayaking and canoeing are also popular, providing opportunities to explore the coastline, secret coves, and the neighbouring Portland Harbour. Guided excursions are provided for people interested in learning about the surrounding marine life and geology while paddling peacefully. Snorkelling and scuba diving are other excellent ways to explore Weymouth's underwater environment, with several dive sites rich with marine life and interesting shipwrecks.

Cycling and Walking Trails

Weymouth's stunning landscapes and seaside trails make it an ideal location for cycling and walking lovers. Whether you prefer a leisurely stroll, a strenuous trek, or a gorgeous bike ride, Weymouth has pathways to suit every taste and fitness level.

The Rodwell Trail is popular with both hikers and cyclists. This disused railway line has been restored into a magnificent two-mile trail that connects Weymouth to the Isle of Portland. The route provides stunning views of the coastline while passing through natural reserves and historic landmarks, making it both entertaining and instructive.

For a more difficult climb, the South West Coast Path offers breathtaking vistas of the Jurassic Coast. This National Trail spans 630 miles along the coast, from Minehead in Somerset to Poole Harbour in Dorset. The area around Weymouth contains a combination of stunning cliffs, sandy beaches, and lovely settlements. It's ideal for a day trek or a longer trip, with lots of opportunities to pause and admire the stunning surroundings.

Cycling lovers will appreciate the wide range of routes accessible in and around Weymouth. The Weymouth to Abbotsbury cycling route is a pleasant 10-mile ride over undulating farmland, with the option of continuing your adventure to the quaint town of Abbotsbury, noted for its swannery and subtropical gardens. The Portland Circuit, a

13-mile loop around the Isle of Portland, provides a more demanding ride with spectacular coastline vistas and some steep climbs.

Fishing Spots

Weymouth is an angler's paradise, with a variety of fishing chances from the shore, pier, and boat. Whether you are an expert fisherman or a first-time angler, Weymouth's varied waterways are alive with fish and offer a pleasant experience.

Shore fishing is popular around beaches and harbours, where you may catch fish including bass, flounder, and mackerel. The Stone Pier is a popular destination for both locals and visitors, offering convenient access and the opportunity to catch a variety of fish. Local businesses sell fishing equipment and bait, and skilled fishermen are available to offer tips and advice.

Boat fishing cruises departing from Weymouth Harbour are available for those seeking to travel further out. These charters cater to all skill levels and provide the opportunity to capture bigger species such as cod, pollock, and conger eel. Full-day and half-day excursions are offered, with some boats providing all essential equipment and direction.

Freshwater fishing is also available in the surrounding lakes and rivers. Lodmoor Country Park includes a well-stocked fishing lake, ideal for a relaxing day of angling in a picturesque environment. Whether you enjoy the excitement of deep-sea fishing or the peacefulness of freshwater fishing, Weymouth has something for everyone.

Golf Courses

Golf fans can discover many good courses in and around Weymouth that provide difficult play and breathtaking vistas. Whether you're a seasoned golfer or a beginner, the area's golf courses provide a great chance to enjoy the outdoors while also improving your game.

The Weymouth Golf Club, only a short drive from the town centre, is a well-kept 18-hole course that welcomes guests. The course is noted for its welcoming environment, picturesque parkland setting, and demanding layout. Golfers may enjoy a game of golf followed by refreshments at the clubhouse, which has a friendly atmosphere and great views of the course.

The Isle of Purbeck Golf Club, located near Weymouth, provides two courses: an 18-hole championship course and a 9-hole course. The courses are placed against the background of the Jurassic Coast, with stunning views of the sea and surrounding countryside. The championship course is especially demanding, with undulating fairways and carefully positioned bunkers.

Wessex Golf Centre provides a more relaxing atmosphere, with a 9-hole, par-3 course ideal for novices and families. The facility also has a driving range, putting green, and expert instruction, making it an excellent location for golfers of all ages and ability levels to practise and develop their game.

Whether you enjoy the challenge of a full 18-hole course or a more leisurely game on a lesser course, Weymouth's golf options appeal to all tastes. The picturesque landscapes and inviting clubs guarantee that all guests have a wonderful golfing experience.

In conclusion, Weymouth's outdoor activities offer several opportunities to appreciate the town's natural beauty and different landscapes. From thrilling watersports and gorgeous bicycle paths to calm fishing locations and picturesque golf courses, there is something for everyone to enjoy. Accept the outdoors and explore the various thrills that await you in Weymouth.

Hidden Gems

Weymouth is full with well-known sites that attract people from all over, but it also hides a number of lesser-known gems that provide unique experiences and peaceful moments of exploration. These hidden jewels, which are sometimes ignored by casual tourists, offer a closer connection to the town's history, natural beauty, and local character. Let's reveal some of Weymouth's best-kept secrets.

Sandsfoot Gardens

Sandsfoot Gardens, located near the ancient ruins of Sandsfoot Castle, provides a tranquil respite with beautifully planted gardens and breathtaking views of Portland Harbour. This hidden treasure is a serene location ideal for a pleasant stroll or a relaxing afternoon. The well-kept grounds include vivid flower beds, groomed lawns, and covered resting areas where you can unwind and take in the scenery.

The panoramic view of the harbour and the Isle of Portland is without a doubt Sandsfoot Gardens' centrepiece. The grounds are ideal for having a picnic, reading a book, or simply relaxing in the sun. Seasonal blossoms and well-placed seats entice visitors to stay and admire the beauty of this peaceful area of Weymouth. The closeness to Sandsfoot Castle adds a layer of historical mystery, making it an enjoyable place to explore.

Jordan Hill Roman Temple

For history buffs, the Jordan Hill Roman Temple is a fascinating landmark that provides insight into Weymouth's ancient past. This archeological monument, located on a hill overlooking Bowleaze Cove, dates back to the 4th century AD and is thought to have served as a place of worship for local Roman residents.

Despite their small size, the temple ruins hold historical significance. Informational plaques explain the temple's history and the Roman presence in Weymouth, allowing visitors to envision what life could have been like during that time. The site's lofty elevation provides breathtaking views of the surrounding countryside and ocean, making it an ideal spot for a short stroll or leisurely walk.

Exploring the Jordan Hill Roman Temple is both an informative experience and a relaxing getaway. The hill's peaceful and solitary character creates a sense of tranquillity, allowing visitors to ponder on the site's historical significance while admiring the natural beauty of the surrounding.

Preston Beach Road Nature Reserve

The Preston Beach Road Nature Reserve, located between the busy town of Weymouth and the village of Preston, is a hidden gem of wildlife and natural beauty. This coastal reserve is ideal for birdwatchers, wildlife enthusiasts, and anybody looking for a calm retreat from the bustling seaside.

The reserve has a variety of habitats, including salt marshes, reed beds, and shingle beaches, which support a broad diversity of plant and wildlife. Walking routes and boardwalks weave through the area, allowing visitors to study the native species up close. Birds such as oystercatchers, lapwings, and numerous duck and wader species may be observed all year, making it an ideal place for birding.

Interpretive signs explain the reserve's ecology and the necessity of protecting these coastal ecosystems. The tranquil ambiance and soft sounds of nature offer a relaxing environment ideal for a leisurely walk or a quiet period of introspection. The Preston Beach Road Nature Reserve is a hidden gem worth discovering, showcasing Weymouth's ecological richness.

Stone Pier

While the crowded Weymouth Harbour is a well-known destination, the Stone Pier provides a more relaxed yet equally attractive experience. The Stone Pier, which extends out into the harbour, provides a calm area to take in the marine landscape, watch vessels come and go, and enjoy the soft sea wind.

This hidden gem is famous among local fishermen, who frequently line the pier in search of a nice catch. For tourists, it's an excellent area to try your hand at fishing or simply observe the activities around you. The pier's location provides stunning views of the town, port, and open sea, making it ideal for photography or a leisurely beach stroll.

The Stone Pier is also an excellent spot to see the sunset, as the evening light casts a golden glow over the ocean and town. The murmur of the waves and the occasional call of seagulls contribute to the pier's peaceful atmosphere. Whether you're searching for a peaceful location to unwind or a gorgeous area to take in Weymouth's coastal splendour, the Stone Pier is a hidden gem not to be overlooked.

In conclusion, Weymouth's hidden treasures provide unique and gratifying experiences away from the more congested tourist destinations. Sandsfoot Gardens, Jordan Hill Roman Temple, Preston Beach Road Nature Reserve, and the Stone Pier all provide unique glimpses into the town's natural beauty, historical significance, and local character. Exploring these lesser-known jewels will enrich your vacation and reveal a side of Weymouth that is genuinely unique.

Family-Friendly Attractions

Weymouth is an excellent family destination, with a wide range of attractions to suit all ages. Whether you're looking for educational activities, exhilarating rides, or engaging entertainment, Weymouth has something for the whole family. Here are some of the best family attractions for a fun and memorable vacation.

Sea-Life Adventure Park

The Sea species Adventure Park is a must-see for families, providing an immersive and informative experience that puts you face to face with marine species from across the world. This aquarium, located in Lodmoor Country Park, has a variety of exhibits and interactive displays that will attract both children and adults.

As you tour the park, you'll come across many themed zones, each presenting a distinct aquatic ecosystem and its creatures. From the vivid hues of coral reefs to the deep depths of the ocean, there is something for everyone to enjoy. Highlights include the Ocean Tunnel, where visitors may travel through an underwater tunnel surrounded by sharks, rays, and tropical fish, and Penguin Island, which is home to a lively colony of Humboldt penguins.

Throughout the day, the park also provides entertaining presentations and feeding demonstrations, giving visitors unique insights into the animals' lives and behaviours. Hands-on experiences, like the touch pool, allow youngsters to get up close and personal with starfish, crabs, and other sea animals.

In addition to its aquatic exhibits, the Sea Life Adventure Park offers a range of outdoor activities such as a splash play area, mini-golf, and adventure playground. With so much to see and do, the park is an excellent choice for a fun-filled family outing.

Fantasy Island Fun Park

Fantasy Island Fun Park is a family amusement park that offers thrill and pleasure to guests of all ages. Located on Bowleaze Cove, this lovely park has a variety of rides and activities for both children and adults.

The park offers a variety of classic amusement attractions, such as bumper cars, a carousel, and a Ferris wheel, making it enjoyable for the entire family. For smaller children, there are moderate rides like little trains and teacups to ensure that even the youngest guests have a good time. Thrill-seekers will like the park's most challenging attractions, which include roller coasters and spinning rides that provide an adrenaline boost.

In addition to the attractions, Fantasy Island Fun Park has an arcade with games and prizes, a soft play area for infants, and a café that serves drinks and snacks. The park's seaside position offers breathtaking views of the sea, giving it an idyllic setting for a day of fun and laughter.

Seasonal events and themed days enhance the park's appeal, providing unique activities and entertainment throughout the year. Whether you're riding the Ferris wheel, playing arcade games, or having an ice cream by the water, Fantasy Island Fun Park is a great place for families looking for a day of fun and adventure.

Weymouth Pavilion

Weymouth Pavilion is a cultural hub that provides a variety of entertainment opportunities for families. This historic facility on the beachfront accommodates a wide range of acts, including theatre plays, concerts, comedy shows, and family events.

The Pavilion's schedule offers something for everyone, with performances suitable for all ages. Family events, such as pantomimes, children's theatre, and magic shows, are entertaining and participatory for young audiences. The theatre also organises musical acts, ranging from classical concerts to modern bands, so there is something for everyone's taste.

In addition to its main auditorium, the Pavilion has a smaller theatre area and a café bar that serves refreshments and provides a relaxing ambiance before or after the event. The venue's coastal position makes it an ideal stop for a day out in Weymouth, allowing families to watch a show before exploring the local beach and promenade.

Special activities, such as seminars and themed parties, contribute to the Pavilion's family-friendly atmosphere. Whether you're seeing a thrilling theatre show or singing along at a family concert, Weymouth Pavilion offers unforgettable entertainment experiences for people of every age.

Pirate Adventure Mini Golf

For a swashbuckling good time, visit Pirate Adventure Mini Golf, a themed miniature golf course that offers fun and excitement for the entire family. This activity on the seaside mixes the difficulty of mini-golf with the thrill of a pirate-themed adventure.

The 18-hole course has inventive pirate-themed hazards including shipwrecks, treasure chests, and falling waterfalls. Each hole delivers a new challenge, asking players to manoeuvre around hazards while aiming for the coveted hole-in-one. The course's unique design and attention to detail make it a fun and engaging experience for both children and adults.

Pirate Adventure Mini Golf is an excellent way to spend quality time with your family, with lots of opportunity for friendly rivalry and fun. The course's coastal position creates a lovely backdrop, enabling you to enjoy the fresh sea air and breathtaking vistas while playing.

In addition to the mini-golf course, the location has a café that serves food and refreshments, as well as a seating area where you can relax and watch other players complete the game. Whether you're a seasoned player or a beginner, Pirate Adventure Mini Golf provides a fun and memorable experience for families visiting Weymouth.

Finally, Weymouth's family-friendly attractions provide a variety of activities suitable for guests of all ages. There is no shortage of fun and excitement for kids in Weymouth, with instructive exhibitions at Sea Life Adventure Park and exciting rides at Fantasy Island Fun Park, as well as diverse concerts at Weymouth Pavilion and the amusing challenges of Pirate Adventure Mini Golf. Explore these beautiful sites and enjoy a range of activities while making great memories with your loved ones.

Shopping in Weymouth

Weymouth provides a lovely shopping experience that combines historic charm, local products, high-street brands, and distinctive small stores. Whether you're searching for souvenirs, fresh fruit, or a unique present, Weymouth's retail district has something for everyone. Let's look at some of the top spots to shop in this seaside town.

Brewer's Quay

Brewers Quay is a historic structure that has been turned into a thriving commerce and cultural destination. Located in the heart of Weymouth's old town, this attractive location blends historical beauty with a range of modern delights.

Specialty Stores: Brewers Quay is home to a variety of specialty stores that sell antiques, collectibles, and unique gifts. Vintage apparel and jewellery are available, as well as home décor and art items.

Craft Workshops: Many of the stores on Brewers Quay provide craft workshops and demonstrations. Visitors may learn new talents, like ceramics or painting, and make their own handcrafted mementos.

Cafés & Restaurants: After a day of shopping, unwind at one of the quiet cafés or restaurants on Brewers Quay. Enjoy a cup of coffee, a small meal, or a delectable dessert while taking in the historic atmosphere.

Weymouth Farmers' Market

The Weymouth Farmers' Market is a must-see for everyone who likes fresh, locally grown products. The market, which is held on a monthly basis at various places across town, provides a colourful ambiance as well as an opportunity to support local farmers and artists.

Fresh Produce: The market's stalls are stocked with fresh fruits and vegetables, organic meats, dairy products, and freshly baked goodies. It's the ideal spot to buy up supplies for a picnic or a homemade supper.

Local Specialties: Try Dorset cheeses, honey, jams, and handcrafted chocolates. These delightful delicacies make great presents or keepsakes.

Artisan Products: In addition to food, the market has vendors offering handcrafted products such as ceramics, textiles, jewellery, and woodwork. These one-of-a-kind goods showcase local craftsmen' ability and ingenuity.

The market is more than simply a shopping destination; it is also a gathering area for the community. Enjoy live music, talk to the exhibitors, and take in the cheerful, welcoming ambiance.

High-Street Shopping

Weymouth's main street combines big retail brands with local shops, making for a convenient and delightful shopping experience.

Fashion & Accessories: Check out the newest fashion and accessory trends from well-known retailers including Marks & Spencer, H&M, and New Look. There is a diverse selection of apparel, shoes, and accessories to suit all ages and preferences.

Beauty & Health: There are various beauty and health retailers on the high street, including Boots and Superdrug. You'll discover everything you need in one spot, including skincare items, cosmetics, and health supplements.

Books & Stationery: For book enthusiasts, WHSmith and Waterstones have an excellent assortment of books, periodicals, and stationery. These stores provide everything you need, whether you're looking for the current bestseller or a one-of-a-kind diary.

Electronics & Gadgets: Stores such as Currys PC World sell a wide selection of electronics and gadgets, from the newest smartphones and laptops to home appliances and gaming consoles.

Independent Boutiques & Artisan Shops

Weymouth has a diverse range of small boutiques and artisan businesses, each offering something distinctive and unique.

Clothing Boutiques: Independent clothing businesses provide attractive and distinctive fashion things that you won't find in major retailers. These businesses frequently sell locally made apparel and accessories.

Artisan Crafts: Discover artisan stores that sell handcrafted items including pottery, glassware, and textiles. These finely created objects would make excellent gifts or complements to your home decor.

Gourmet Food Shops: Visit gourmet food establishments that specialise in both local and foreign delicacies. From premium wines and cheeses to handcrafted chocolates and preserves, you'll discover a variety of gourmet delicacies to please your palate.

Gift Stores: Weymouth's independent gift stores sell a wide range of one-of-a-kind and unusual products that make ideal mementos or gifts. Browse handcrafted jewellery, aromatic candles, and locally created bath items.

In summary, Weymouth's shops and markets offer a variety and rewarding experience for all tourists. Whether you're strolling along the historic Brewers Quay, shopping for fresh vegetables at the Farmers' Market, enjoying the diversity of the main street, or discovering unusual items in independent shops, you'll appreciate the combination of local character and modern convenience. Happy shopping!

Food and Drink

Weymouth's culinary culture is a lovely combination of classic Dorset cuisines, contemporary eating experiences, and lively food events. Whether you're a gourmet seeking to experience local delicacies or simply searching for a fantastic location to dine and drink, Weymouth offers something for you. Here's a list of the top food and beverage experiences in this picturesque seaside town.

Traditional Dorset Cuisine

Dorset's culinary tradition is rich and diverse, reflecting the region's agricultural abundance and seaside gems.

Dorset Apple Cake: A popular regional delicacy cooked with local apples and frequently seasoned with cinnamon and nutmeg. It is normally served warm, with a dab of clotted cream.

Blue Vinny Cheese: This traditional blue cheese is peculiar to Dorset. It is created with unpasteurized cow's milk and has a crumbly texture and unique flavour. Enjoy it with crackers or as part of a cheese platter.

Dorset Knobs: These firm, dry biscuits prepared from bread dough can be paired with cheese or dipped in tea. They are a local curiosity and must-try for anyone seeking a unique experience.

Seafood: As a seaside town, Weymouth has an abundance of fresh fish. Local staples such as mackerel, crab, and lobster are frequently served simply to accentuate their natural tastes.

Best Restaurants and Cafés

Weymouth has a diverse eating scene, ranging from fine dining to intimate cafés, all of which provide wonderful meals and provide pleasant service.

The Crab House Café: Known for its delicious seafood and friendly environment, provides breathtaking views of Chesil Beach. The menu varies daily to reflect the catch of the day, assuring the freshest foods.

Marlboro Restaurant: This renowned establishment is known for its classic fish and chips. This British staple, cooked with locally sourced fish, is best enjoyed near the harbour.

The George Bar & Grill: Located on the harborside, provides a range of grilled meats, seafood, and vegetarian meals. Its outdoor dining area provides stunning views of the bay.

The Boat Café: For a small lunch or a coffee break, The Boat Café provides a delightful location directly on the beach. Enjoy sandwiches, salads, and handmade sweets while admiring the sea views.

Best Pubs & Bars

Weymouth's pubs and bars are ideal for unwinding with a drink and taking in the local vibe. Whether you're looking for a pint of local ale or a handmade cocktail, there's something for you.

The Old Rooms Inn: Located near the waterfront, this old bar has a welcoming ambiance. It provides a wide selection of local ales, ciders, and classic pub cuisine. The outside dining area is perfect for viewing the boats arriving and going.

The Ship Inn: This bustling pub, located near the waterfront, is recognized for its extensive range of beers and ales, as well as its robust food. Live music and quiz nights add to the enjoyment, making it popular with both residents and visitors.

The Nook Cocktail Club: For a more modern atmosphere, The Nook Cocktail Club serves a diverse selection of unique drinks. The modern décor and courteous personnel make it an ideal spot for an evening out.

The Dorset Burger Company: The Dorset Burger Company combines the best of both worlds, serving gourmet burgers as well as craft beers and beverages. It's an ideal location for a relaxed supper with friends or family.

Food Festivals & Events

Weymouth has a number of food festivals and events throughout the year that highlight local produce and culinary ability.

Weymouth Seafood Festival: Held every July, this festival honours the town's fishing tradition. Along the scenic harborside, you may see culinary demos, buy fresh seafood, and listen to live music.

Dorset Knob Throwing Festival: This eccentric festival, held in adjacent Cattistock, has a range of knob-themed activities and competitions, as well as local food and drink booths. It's an enjoyable day out for the entire family.

Weymouth Farmers' Market: This regular market offers an excellent opportunity to taste and purchase local products directly from farmers and producers. Fresh fruits, vegetables, meat, cheese, and baked products are all available.

Food & Drink Trails: Throughout the year, several trails and excursions are planned to showcase local producers and allow tourists to taste Dorset's gastronomic offerings. These trips sometimes include visits to farms, breweries, and artisanal crafts.

Finally, Weymouth's food and drink scene is diversified, with options ranging from traditional Dorset delicacies to modern gourmet experiences. Whether you're dining at a high-end restaurant, drinking a pint at a small pub, or attending a food festival, Weymouth's culinary choices are as welcome and diverse as its breathtaking coastline.

Cultural Experiences

Weymouth is more than simply a picturesque beach town; it is also a thriving centre of cultural events and experiences. From exciting festivals to rich cultural traditions and intriguing historical excursions, there is always something to engage and inspire tourists. Here's a look at some of Weymouth's top cultural experiences.

Weymouth Carnival

The Weymouth Carnival is one of the most popular events of the year, attracting both locals and tourists for a day of fun and community spirit. Every summer, the carnival is a lively event that includes a range of activities and entertainment.

Parade: The big procession, which makes its way across town, is the carnival's main attraction. Colourful floats, marching bands, dancing troupes, and costumed performers make for a colourful and enjoyable show. Each year, the parade features a different theme, which adds to the excitement and ingenuity.

Live Entertainment: Throughout the day, numerous stages around town present live performances in music, dance, and drama. Local musicians, choirs, and dance organisations perform for all ages.

Funfair & Stalls: The carnival has a funfair with rides and games, as well as a variety of booths offering food, beverages, crafts, and souvenirs. It's an excellent opportunity to sample local cuisine and get one-of-a-kind souvenirs.

Fireworks: The carnival finishes with a stunning fireworks show over the bay, which illuminates the night sky in a brilliant kaleidoscope of colours. It's the ideal way to cap off a day of celebration and fun.

Dorset Seafood Festival

The Dorset Seafood Festival is another highlight of Weymouth's cultural calendar, showcasing the area's strong marine tradition and culinary brilliance. The event, which takes place yearly on the harborside, is a must-see for foodies.

Seafood Booths: The event includes a variety of booths serving fresh seafood produced by local chefs and sellers. From crab and lobster to oysters and mussels, there's something for every seafood lover's taste.

Culinary Demos: Renowned chefs from throughout the area do live culinary demos. Visitors may learn new recipes and methods while tasting tasty foods created on the spot.

Educational Presentations: The festival also features enlightening presentations on sustainable fishing techniques, marine conservation, and the value of supporting local fisheries. It provides a chance to learn about the efforts being done to protect the maritime environment.

Family Activities: The Dorset Seafood Festival offers activities and entertainment for children, such as face painting, storytelling, and hands-on cookery lessons. It's an excellent method to expose young children to the pleasures of seafood and cooking.

Local Arts and Music Scene

Weymouth has a lively local art and music scene, with several galleries, live music venues, and cultural events held throughout the year.

Art Galleries: Visit local art galleries such as The Leighton Art Gallery and Art Asylum. These galleries include local artists' works, which range from paintings and sculptures to photography and mixed media. Exhibitions vary often, presenting new and different creative ideas.

Live Music: Weymouth has a thriving music culture, with live performances taking place at places including The Pavilion and local pubs. From rock bands and jazz ensembles to folk singers and classical performers, there is always something to appreciate. The town frequently holds music festivals, which bring together outstanding performers from both close and far.

Community Events: Local community centres and cultural hubs commonly host events such as craft fairs, open mic nights, and art classes. These events showcase local talent and allow visitors to connect with the creative community.

Historical Tours and Walks

Weymouth's rich history may be discovered through a number of historic excursions and walks that provide insight into the town's past and cultural heritage.

Guided Walking Tours: Take a guided walking tour around Weymouth's historic monuments and learn about its intriguing history. Knowledgeable guides bring history to life by telling stories about the town's maritime origins, position in the Georgian and Victorian eras, and noteworthy personalities who influenced its growth.

Self-Guided Tours: Local tourist information centres can provide self-guided tour maps to individuals who want to explore at their own leisure. These maps highlight significant historical landmarks and give contextual information about each location.

History Trails: Weymouth has various history trails that lead tourists through historic locations such as the Old Harbour, Nothe Fort, and town centre. These well-marked pathways offer a comprehensive view of the town's cultural and historical landscape.

Historical Re-enactments: Throughout the summer, historical reenactments and living history activities are frequently staged at sites such as the Nothe Fort. These events include costumed performers, historical displays, and participatory activities that take guests back in time.

In summary, Weymouth's cultural experiences provide a rich and diverse tapestry of events that honour the town's heritage, creative skill, and community spirit. Whether you're dancing at the carnival, eating fresh seafood, discovering local art, or taking a history tour, Weymouth's cultural offers are as compelling and diverse as its stunning scenery.

Day Trips from Weymouth

Weymouth's position on the breathtaking Jurassic Coast gives it an ideal base for exploring the surrounding area. There are several exciting day tours to choose from, including gorgeous coastal vistas, ancient villages, and one-of-a-kind animal encounters. Here are some great places to visit for a memorable day out.

Portland Bill and Lighthouse

Anyone visiting Weymouth should go to Portland Bill and see the magnificent lighthouse. Located on the Isle of Portland, just a short drive from Weymouth, this spectacular headland provides stunning coastline vistas as well as an insight into maritime history.

Portland Bill Lighthouse: For more than a century, this lighthouse has stood tall on the southern tip of the Isle of Portland, guiding sailors safely over the hazardous waters of the English Channel. Visitors may join a guided tour to learn about the lighthouse's history, see its numerous rooms, and admire the panoramic views from the top.

Coastal Walks: The rough coastline surrounding Portland Bill is ideal for strolling and exploring. Several well-marked routes provide breathtaking views of the sea, cliffs, and unusual rock formations. Keep a watch out for local wildlife, which includes seagulls and the occasional seal.

Pulpit Rock: This spectacular rock structure, located near the lighthouse, is a favourite photo location and provides a dramatic background for your visit. Climbing up the rock offers an excellent vantage point for taking in the surrounding area.

Quaint Cafés: After touring the region, unwind at one of the surrounding cafés, which serve a variety of refreshments, from freshly baked cakes to hearty meals, all while taking in the breathtaking sea views.

Chesil Beach

Chesil Beach is one of the most iconic and distinctive natural features in the United Kingdom. This 18-mile-long pebble beach extends from West Bay to the Isle of Portland, separated from the mainland by the Fleet Lagoon.

Scenic Beauty: The huge expanse of stones, along with the sound of waves breaking on the coast, creates a captivating and serene scene. It's ideal for a relaxing walk or a picnic by the water.

Birdwatching: The Fleet Lagoon, located behind Chesil Beach, is a sanctuary for birdwatchers. It is a Special Protection Area that supports a diverse range of bird species, including wading birds and waterfowl. Bring your binoculars and spend the day studying animals in this beautiful environment.

Fishing: Chesil Beach is a famous fishing area due to its abundant marine life. Anglers may expect to catch a wide range of species, including mackerel, bass, and flatfish. Whether you're a seasoned fisherman or a beginner, the beach provides an excellent opportunity to enjoy this pleasant activity.

Jurassic Coast: Chesil Beach, part of the UNESCO World Heritage-listed Jurassic Coast, provides an opportunity to learn about the area's geological history. For people of all ages, fossil searching and beachcombing may be both enjoyable and informative.

Dorchester

Dorchester, the mediaeval county town of Dorset, is only a short drive from Weymouth and has a plethora of cultural and historical attractions.

Roman Town House: Explore the remnants of this spectacular Roman mansion from the fourth century. The site features well-preserved mosaic floors and offers an intriguing glimpse into Roman life in Britain.

Dorset County Museum: This museum celebrates Dorset's rich history and traditions, with exhibits ranging from ancient periods to the present. Highlights include displays about local geology and archeology, as well as Thomas Hardy's life and works.

Maiden Castle: Located just outside of Dorchester, is one of Europe's largest and most intricate Iron Age hill forts. Wander over the historic walls and enjoy the breathtaking views of the surrounding landscape.

Borough Gardens: Spend a leisurely afternoon in the wonderfully kept Borough Gardens. These Victorian gardens, which include flower beds, a bandstand, and a children's play area, provide a tranquil escape in the centre of town.

Abbotsbury Swannery

A visit to Abbotsbury Swannery is an unforgettable and magical experience. This swannery, around 10 miles from Weymouth, is the only spot in the world where you may stroll among a colony of breeding mute swans.

Swan Feeding: One of the attractions of a trip to Abbotsbury Swannery is the chance to help feed the swans. Scheduled feeding times allow guests to get up close and personal with these gorgeous birds while learning about their habits and lifecycle from expert personnel.

Nature Trails: The swannery is located in a wonderful natural area, with various walking routes that enable you to explore the surrounding countryside and enjoy breathtaking views of the Fleet Lagoon and Chesil Beach.

Family Activities: Abbotsbury Swannery has a variety of family-friendly activities such as a labyrinth, play area, and seasonal events. It's a wonderful choice for a fun and instructive day out with the kids.

Subtropical Gardens: While at Abbotsbury, make time to explore the adjacent Abbotsbury Subtropical Gardens. These award-winning gardens contain a diverse collection of exotic plants and trees, resulting in a lush and bright paradise.

Finally, the areas around Weymouth provide a broad range of day outings catering to all interests, including natural beauty, wildlife, history, and culture. Whether you're exploring the majestic coastline at Portland Bill, traversing the pebbled stretch of Chesil Beach, digging into Dorchester's ancient treasures, or experiencing the distinct charm of Abbotsbury Swannery, these day adventures will enhance your time in Weymouth and leave you with memorable memories.

Travel Tips

Making the most of your visit to Weymouth involves more than just knowing where to go and what to see. Practical travel tips can enhance your experience, ensuring a smooth and enjoyable stay. Here's a guide to navigating Weymouth, staying safe and healthy, understanding local customs, and practising sustainable tourism.

Navigating Weymouth

Weymouth is a compact and walkable town, but knowing the best ways to get around can save you time and enhance your visit.

Walking: The best way to explore Weymouth is on foot. Many of the town's attractions, including the beach, harbour, and town centre, are within walking distance of each other. Comfortable shoes and a good map or GPS app will help you navigate easily.

Public Transport: Weymouth is serviced by a reliable bus network, with regular routes connecting key areas of the town and surrounding regions. The Jurassic Coaster bus service is particularly useful for exploring the Jurassic Coast. Bus schedules and tickets are available online or at local stations.

Cycling: Weymouth is bicycle-friendly, with several bike rental shops and dedicated cycling paths. Cycling is a great way to see more of the town and its scenic surroundings, such as the Rodwell Trail and the routes along the coast.

Driving: If you prefer to drive, Weymouth has ample parking options, including public car parks and street parking. Be mindful of parking regulations and charges. Driving is convenient for day trips to nearby attractions like Portland Bill and Dorchester.

Taxis & Rideshares: Taxis are readily available in Weymouth, with several local companies offering services. Ridesharing services like Uber also operate in the area, providing another convenient option for getting around.

Health and Safety

Staying healthy and safe during your visit to Weymouth is paramount. Here are some essential tips to keep in mind:

Emergency Services: In case of emergency, dial 999 for police, fire, or medical assistance. For non-emergency medical help, dial 111.

Medical Facilities: Weymouth has several pharmacies, GP practices, and the Weymouth Community Hospital for minor injuries and illnesses. For more serious health issues, Dorchester's Dorset County Hospital is nearby.

Beach Safety: When visiting the beach, follow safety guidelines. Swim in designated areas patrolled by lifeguards, observe warning flags, and avoid swimming alone. Be cautious of tides and currents.

Sun Protection: Protect yourself from the sun by wearing sunscreen, hats, and sunglasses. Drink plenty of water to stay hydrated, especially during the summer months.

Personal Safety: Weymouth is generally safe, but it's wise to take standard precautions. Keep an eye on your belongings, especially in crowded areas, and avoid walking alone in secluded areas at night.

Local Customs and Etiquette

Understanding local customs and etiquette can enrich your experience and help you connect with the community.

Politeness: The British are known for their politeness. Use phrases like "please," "thank you," and "excuse me" in your interactions. A friendly greeting and a smile go a long way.

Queueing: Queuing (standing in line) is a common practice in the UK. Always wait your turn in lines at shops, bus stops, and other public places.

Tipping: Tipping is customary in restaurants, cafés, and for taxi drivers. A tip of 10-15% is standard in restaurants if service is not included. Tipping in pubs is not expected, but rounding up to the nearest pound is appreciated.

Respect for Nature: Respect the natural beauty of Weymouth by not littering and following guidelines for protecting local wildlife and habitats. Stick to marked paths in nature reserves and parks.

Conversation: Engage in light and friendly conversation. Topics like the weather, local attractions, and shared interests are good conversation starters. Avoid discussing politics and religion unless you know the other person well.

Sustainable Tourism Practices

Practising sustainable tourism ensures that Weymouth remains beautiful and welcoming for future generations.

Reduce Waste: Minimise waste by using reusable bags, bottles, and containers. Dispose of rubbish responsibly and recycle whenever possible.

Eco-Friendly Transport: Opt for walking, cycling, or public transport to reduce your carbon footprint. Consider carpooling or using electric vehicles if you need to drive.

Support Local Businesses: Eat at local restaurants, shop at independent stores, and stay at locally-owned accommodations. Supporting local businesses helps the community thrive.

Conserve Resources: Be mindful of your water and energy usage. Turn off lights and electronics when not in use, and avoid wasting water.

Wildlife Respect: Respect local wildlife by observing from a distance and not disturbing their natural habitats. Follow guidelines in nature reserves and parks to protect plants and animals.

Cultural Respect: Show respect for Weymouth's cultural heritage by preserving historic sites and monuments. Avoid touching or defacing any structures and adhere to posted guidelines.

In conclusion, by following these travel tips, you can ensure a smooth, enjoyable, and respectful visit to Weymouth. Navigating the town with ease, staying safe and healthy, understanding local customs, and practising sustainable tourism will enhance your experience and help preserve this beautiful destination for future visitors.

Seasonal Activities

Weymouth is a year-round destination with each season offering its own unique charm and activities. Whether you enjoy the warmth of summer, the crisp air of autumn, the festive spirit of winter, or the blooming beauty of spring, there's always something special to do. Here's a guide to the best seasonal activities in Weymouth.

Summer Beach Activities

Summer in Weymouth is all about soaking up the sun and enjoying the town's stunning coastline.

Swimming and Sunbathing: Weymouth Beach is a perfect spot for swimming and sunbathing. The sandy shore and safe, shallow waters make it ideal for families. Lifeguards are on duty during peak times to ensure safety.

Beach Sports: Engage in beach sports such as volleyball, football, and frisbee. The designated sports areas on Weymouth Beach are great for friendly matches and keeping active.

Paddleboarding & Kayaking: Explore the calm waters of Weymouth Bay with paddle boarding or kayaking. Equipment can be rented from local shops, and there are lessons available for beginners.

Boat Trips: Take a boat trip along the Jurassic Coast to see the stunning cliffs and rock formations from the water. Options include guided tours, fishing trips, and scenic cruises.

Beachfront Entertainment: Enjoy live music, beachside cafes, and ice cream parlours along the promenade. Weymouth hosts various events and entertainment on the beach during the summer, making it a lively place to spend your days and evenings.

Autumn Hiking Trails

Autumn brings cooler temperatures and vibrant foliage, making it an excellent time for hiking and exploring Weymouth's natural beauty.

South West Coast Path: This famous coastal trail offers stunning views of the Jurassic Coast. The section from Weymouth to Durdle Door is particularly scenic, with dramatic cliffs, coves, and rolling countryside.

Radipole Lake Nature Reserve: Enjoy a peaceful walk through this urban nature reserve. The trails are well-maintained, and the autumn colours add a picturesque backdrop. Birdwatchers will delight in the variety of species that visit during this season.

Nothe Gardens: These historic gardens offer lovely walking paths with views over Weymouth Bay and the harbour. The autumn foliage adds a colourful touch to the gardens, making it a pleasant place for a leisurely stroll.

Hardy's Monument: Hike up to Hardy's Monument for panoramic views of the Dorset countryside. The trails leading to the monument are surrounded by heather and gorse, which are particularly beautiful in autumn.

Winter Festivities

Winter in Weymouth is filled with festive cheer and cosy activities to enjoy with family and friends.

Christmas Markets: Weymouth's Christmas markets are a highlight of the winter season. Browse stalls selling festive foods, handmade crafts, and holiday gifts. The atmosphere is warm and inviting, with twinkling lights and seasonal music.

Weymouth Pavilion Pantomime: The annual pantomime at Weymouth Pavilion is a beloved tradition. These family-friendly shows are full of humour, music, and interactive fun, making them a perfect holiday activity.

Ice Skating: During the winter months, an outdoor ice skating rink is set up in the town centre. It's a great way to enjoy some festive fun, whether you're a seasoned skater or a beginner.

New Year's Eve Fireworks: Ring in the New Year with a spectacular fireworks display over Weymouth Bay. The town comes alive with celebrations, including live music and parties, creating a festive atmosphere to welcome the new year.

Spring Flower Festivals

Spring in Weymouth is a time of renewal and blooming beauty, celebrated through various flower festivals and garden events.

Bennetts Water Gardens: Visit Bennetts Water Gardens in the spring to see the beautiful water lilies in bloom. The gardens also feature a variety of other plants and flowers, making it a perfect spot for a tranquil spring outing.

Abbotsbury Subtropical Gardens: These award-winning gardens host a Spring Flower Festival, showcasing a stunning array of blooms. Wander through the gardens to see magnolias, camellias, and rhododendrons in full bloom.

Greenhill Gardens: These seaside gardens are a riot of colour in the spring. Enjoy a leisurely walk among the flower beds, take in the sea views, and relax in the peaceful surroundings.

Spring Fayres: Local communities often hold spring fayres, featuring plant sales, garden crafts, and local produce. These events are a great way to celebrate the season and support local businesses.

In conclusion, Weymouth offers a rich variety of activities that change with the seasons, ensuring there's always something new and exciting to experience. Whether you're enjoying the sunny beaches in summer, hiking through autumn's colourful trails, participating in winter's festive celebrations, or marvelling at spring's floral displays, each season brings its own unique charm to this beautiful coastal town.

Practical Information

Having practical information at your fingertips can make your stay in Weymouth smooth and stress-free. This chapter provides essential details about useful contacts, emergency services, and local transportation options to help you navigate your visit with ease.

Useful Contacts

Keep these important contacts handy during your stay in Weymouth:

Tourist Information Centre: The Weymouth Tourist Information Centre can provide maps, brochures, and advice on local attractions and events.

- Location: The Royal Arcade, Weymouth DT4 7JE
- Phone: +44 1305 785747
- Email: info@visit-dorset.com

Local Government: For information on local services and amenities, contact the Dorset Council.

- Phone: +44 1305 221000

- Website: www.dorsetcouncil.gov.uk

Taxi Services: Reliable taxi services in Weymouth include:

- Weyline Taxis: +44 1305 777777
- Bee Cars: +44 1305 775151

Healthcare:

- Weymouth Community Hospital: +44 1305 761070
- Dorset County Hospital (Dorchester): +44 1305 251150

Pharmacies:

- Boots Pharmacy: St. Mary St, Weymouth DT4 8PB | +44 1305 783388
- Lloyds Pharmacy: 49 St. Thomas St, Weymouth DT4 8AW | +44 1305 785829

Police Station: For non-emergencies, contact the local police station.

- Address: Radipole Lane, Weymouth DT4 9WW
- Phone: 101 (non-emergency)

Emergency Services

In case of an emergency, knowing how to quickly access help is crucial.

Emergency Numbers

- Police, Fire, Ambulance: 999
- Non-Emergency Medical Help: 111
- Non-Emergency Police: 101

Local Hospitals:

- Weymouth Community Hospital: Melcombe Ave, Weymouth DT4 7TB
- Dorset County Hospital (Dorchester): Williams Ave, Dorchester DT1 2JY

Emergency Preparedness:

- **Location Awareness:** Know your exact location to provide accurate information to emergency services.
- **Medical Information:** Keep a list of any allergies, medications, and medical conditions accessible.
- **Contacts:** Ensure you have contact numbers for family members or travelling companions.

Local Transportation

Understanding the local transportation options can help you get around Weymouth efficiently.

Buses: Weymouth is served by a network of buses that connect the town and surrounding areas. The main bus operator is First Wessex.

- **Popular Routes:**
- Route 1: Weymouth to Portland
- Jurassic Coaster: Weymouth to Bridport, Lyme Regis, and beyond
- **Tickets:** Purchase tickets directly from the driver or via the First Bus app.
- **Timetables:** Available at bus stops, the Tourist Information Centre, or online at www.firstgroup.com.

Trains: Weymouth Railway Station is centrally located and provides connections to major cities, including London, Bristol, and Southampton.

- **Services:** South Western Railway operates regular services to and from Weymouth.
- **Tickets:** Can be purchased at the station, online, or via the South Western Railway app.

- **Timetables:** Available at the station or online at www.southwesternrailway.com.

Taxis & Rideshares: Taxis are readily available and can be booked in advance or hailed on the street.

- **Popular Taxi Companies:**
- Weyline Taxis: +44 1305 777777
- Bee Cars: +44 1305 775151
- Ridesharing services like Uber also operate in Weymouth, providing a convenient option for getting around.

Bicycle Rentals: Weymouth is bike-friendly with several rental shops offering bicycles for exploring the town and coastline.

- **Rental Shops:**
- Jurassic Trails Cycle Hire: Located near the Rodwell Trail, offers a variety of bikes for hire.
- Weymouth Bike Hire: Provides bike rentals and guided cycling tours.

Parking

- **Public Car Parks:** Weymouth has several public car parks with short-term and long-term options.

- Nothe Gardens Car Park: Near Nothe Fort, offers stunning views.
- Swannery Car Park: Centrally located, ideal for town centre access.
- **Street Parking:** Available in various locations; be sure to check signs for any restrictions or charges.

Walking: Weymouth's compact size makes it ideal for exploring on foot. Most attractions, shops, and restaurants are within walking distance.

- **Promenade:** The Esplanade along Weymouth Beach is perfect for a scenic stroll.

In conclusion, having practical information about useful contacts, emergency services, and local transportation can significantly enhance your stay in Weymouth. Being well-prepared ensures that you can navigate the town easily, access help when needed, and make the most of your visit to this beautiful coastal destination.

Sample Itineraries

Planning a trip can be overwhelming, especially with so many attractions and activities to choose from. To help you make the most of your time in Weymouth, we've crafted a variety of detailed itineraries tailored to different types of vacations. Whether you're visiting for a weekend, a week, with family, or for a romantic escape, these itineraries will guide you through a memorable stay in this charming coastal town.

Weekend Getaway Itinerary

A weekend in Weymouth is enough to experience some of the town's best attractions and coastal charm.

Day 1: Arrival and Exploration

Morning: Arrival and Beach Stroll

- Check into your chosen accommodation.
- Start your day with a leisurely stroll along Weymouth Beach, taking in the sea breeze and picturesque views.

Afternoon: Historic Sites and Lunch

- Visit Nothe Fort, a historic sea fort with fascinating exhibits and stunning views over Weymouth Bay.
- Enjoy a seafood lunch at one of the waterfront restaurants in Weymouth Harbour.

Evening: Harbour and Dinner

- Explore Weymouth Harbour, watching the boats and enjoying the lively atmosphere.
- Have dinner at one of the local pubs or restaurants along the harbour.

Day 2: Nature and Heritage

Morning: Gardens and Museums

- Visit Bennetts Water Gardens, where you can enjoy the serene beauty of water lilies and other plant species.
- Head to the Weymouth Museum to learn about the town's rich history and heritage.

Afternoon: Adventure and Lunch

- Take a boat trip along the Jurassic Coast, exploring the dramatic cliffs and unique rock formations.
- Have lunch at a café near the Old Harbour.

Evening: Entertainment and Farewell

- Enjoy a show at the Weymouth Pavilion or stroll along the Esplanade, indulging in an ice cream or fish and chips.
- Bid farewell to Weymouth with a final walk along the beach.

One-Week Adventure Plan

A week in Weymouth allows you to explore the town thoroughly and enjoy some of the surrounding attractions.

Day 1: Welcome to Weymouth

- Settle into your accommodation and take a relaxing walk along Weymouth Beach.
- Enjoy dinner at a local restaurant with views of the sea.

Day 2: Heritage and History

- Visit Nothe Fort in the morning.
- Explore Weymouth Harbour and have lunch at a harborside café.
- Spend the afternoon at the Tudor House Museum, then relax in Nothe Gardens.

Day 3: Coastal Adventures

- Take a day trip to Portland Bill and Lighthouse.
- Explore the rugged coastline and enjoy a picnic lunch.
- Return to Weymouth and dine at a seafood restaurant.

Day 4: Nature and Wildlife

- Visit Lodmoor Country Park, enjoying the trails and nature reserve.
- Head to Radipole Lake Nature Reserve for some birdwatching.
- Have lunch at a local bistro.
- Spend the afternoon at Bennetts Water Gardens.

Day 5: Arts and Culture

- Discover local art at the Leighton Art Gallery.
- Visit Sandsfoot Castle and Gardens.
- Enjoy an afternoon tea at a charming tearoom.
- In the evening, catch a performance at Weymouth Pavilion.

Day 6: Active Pursuits

- Rent a bike and explore the Rodwell Trail.
- Try paddle boarding or kayaking in Weymouth Bay.
- Have lunch at a beachside café.
- Spend the afternoon golfing at one of Weymouth's golf courses.

Day 7: Farewell

- Spend your final morning at the Weymouth Farmers' Market, picking up some local produce and souvenirs.
- Take a last walk along the Esplanade.
- Enjoy a farewell lunch before departing.

Family Vacation Itinerary

Weymouth is a fantastic destination for families, with plenty of attractions and activities to keep everyone entertained.

Day 1: Arrival and Beach Fun

- Check into your family-friendly accommodation.
- Spend the day at Weymouth Beach, building sandcastles, swimming, and enjoying the beach amenities.
- Have dinner at a family-friendly restaurant along the Esplanade.

Day 2: Adventure and Exploration

- Visit the Sea Life Adventure Park in the morning, exploring the marine life exhibits.
- Have lunch at the park's café.
- In the afternoon, head to Fantasy Island Fun Park for rides and games.
- Enjoy dinner at a local pizzeria or diner.

Day 3: Harbour and History

- Explore Weymouth Harbour, taking a boat trip if the weather allows.
- Visit Nothe Fort and its interactive exhibits.

- Have lunch at a harborside café.
- Spend the afternoon at the Pirate Adventure Mini Golf.

Day 4: Nature and Wildlife

- Visit Lodmoor Country Park, enjoying the playground and nature trails.
- Have a picnic lunch in the park.
- Head to Radipole Lake Nature Reserve for some birdwatching and a leisurely walk.

Day 5: Creative and Fun

- Spend the morning at the Tudor House Museum, where kids can learn about history in an engaging way.
- Visit the Leighton Art Gallery and perhaps take part in a family art workshop.
- Enjoy lunch at a family-friendly café.
- Spend the afternoon at Sandsfoot Castle and Gardens, exploring the ruins and beautiful gardens.

Day 6: Relax and Play

- Spend a relaxing morning at Greenhill Gardens.
- Have lunch at a nearby café.

- Spend the afternoon at a nearby leisure centre or swimming pool.

Day 7: Farewell

- Visit the Weymouth Farmers' Market in the morning to pick up some local treats.
- Take a final walk along the beach or the Esplanade.
- Enjoy a farewell lunch before heading home.

Romantic Escape Itinerary

Weymouth's stunning scenery and cosy spots make it an ideal destination for a romantic getaway.

Day 1: Arrival and Sunset Stroll

- Check into your boutique hotel or cosy bed & breakfast.
- Take a romantic sunset stroll along Weymouth Beach.
- Enjoy a candlelit dinner at a waterfront restaurant.

Day 2: Scenic Views and Relaxation

- Spend the morning exploring Nothe Gardens and enjoying the panoramic views.

- Visit Sandsfoot Castle and Gardens, soaking in the historic ambiance.
- Have a picnic lunch in the gardens.
- In the afternoon, take a boat trip along the Jurassic Coast.

Day 3: Arts and Culture

- Visit the Leighton Art Gallery to appreciate local art.
- Take a historic tour of the Tudor House Museum.
- Enjoy afternoon tea at a charming tearoom.
- Spend the evening at a performance at Weymouth Pavilion.

Day 4: Nature and Serenity

- Visit Bennetts Water Gardens, enjoying the peaceful surroundings.
- Head to Greenhill Gardens for a leisurely stroll.
- Have lunch at a seaside café.
- Spend the afternoon relaxing at your accommodation or taking a spa day.

Day 5: Coastal Adventure

- Take a day trip to Portland Bill and Lighthouse.

- Explore the rugged coastline and enjoy a picnic lunch.
- Return to Weymouth for a romantic dinner at a fine dining restaurant.

Day 6: Leisurely Exploration

- Spend a relaxed morning at Weymouth Beach.
- Explore the independent boutiques and artisan shops in town.
- Have lunch at a cosy café.
- Spend the afternoon at Radipole Lake Nature Reserve.

Day 7: Farewell

- Visit the Weymouth Farmers' Market in the morning to pick up some local goodies.
- Take a final romantic walk along the Esplanade.
- Enjoy a farewell lunch before departing.

In conclusion, these itineraries offer a variety of activities tailored to different types of visits, ensuring you make the most of your time in Weymouth. Whether you're here for a weekend, a week, with family, or for a romantic escape,

Weymouth's charm and beauty will make your stay unforgettable.

Conclusion

Weymouth, with its rich blend of history, natural beauty, and vibrant local culture, offers an unparalleled experience for travellers of all kinds. As you've discovered throughout this guide, the town is brimming with iconic landmarks, family-friendly attractions, hidden gems, and a diverse array of outdoor activities. Whether you're strolling along the golden sands of Weymouth Beach, delving into the town's maritime heritage, or exploring the stunning Jurassic Coast, every moment here is a chance to create lasting memories.

The town's historical depth is one of its most compelling features. From the fascinating exhibits at the Weymouth Museum to the ancient remains at Jordan Hill Roman Temple, history enthusiasts will find much to admire. The echoes of the past resonate through landmarks like Nothe Fort and Sandsfoot Castle, painting a vivid picture of Weymouth's storied past.

For nature lovers, Weymouth is a true haven. The serene beauty of Radipole Lake Nature Reserve and the lush expanses of Lodmoor Country Park offer peaceful retreats just a stone's throw from the bustling town centre. Bennetts Water Gardens and Greenhill Gardens provide perfect spots for leisurely walks amidst stunning floral displays and tranquil water features.

Weymouth is also a gateway to adventure. Its watersports and sailing opportunities attract enthusiasts from far and wide, while its cycling and walking trails offer scenic routes through some of Dorset's most beautiful landscapes. Fishing spots and golf courses add to the diverse range of outdoor activities, ensuring there's something for everyone.

Shopping in Weymouth is a delightful experience, with a mix of bustling markets and charming boutiques. The Brewers Quay and Weymouth Farmers' Market offer unique finds and fresh local produce, while the High Street and artisan shops cater to those seeking both mainstream and eclectic treasures.

The culinary scene in Weymouth is another highlight. From traditional Dorset cuisine to contemporary dining experiences, the town's restaurants, cafés, and pubs serve up delicious meals that reflect the region's rich gastronomic heritage. Food festivals and events add an extra layer of enjoyment, allowing visitors to indulge in local flavours and culinary creativity.

Throughout this guide, we've aimed to provide a comprehensive overview of what makes Weymouth a must-visit destination. Its blend of historical significance, natural beauty, and vibrant local culture creates an inviting and dynamic environment that appeals to all types of travellers. Whether you're planning a quick weekend getaway, a week-long adventure, a family vacation, or a romantic escape, Weymouth promises an unforgettable stay.

As you plan your visit, we hope this guide serves as a valuable resource, helping you to explore and appreciate all that Weymouth has to offer. May your time in this charming coastal town be filled with joy, discovery, and wonderful experiences that you'll cherish for years to come. Safe travels, and enjoy your stay in Weymouth.

Printed in Great Britain
by Amazon